# HIGH-FLYING
# PAPER
# AIRPLANES

**E. Richard Churchill**

## STERLING INNOVATION®
An imprint of Sterling Publishing Co., Inc.

New York / London
**www.sterlingpublishing.com**

2  4  6  8  10  9  7  5  3  1

Published by Sterling Publishing Co., Inc.
387 Park Avenue South, New York, NY 10016

This book is comprised of material from the following
Sterling Publishing Co., Inc. titles:
*Fabulous Paper Airplanes* © 1991 by E. Richard Churchill
*Instant Paper Airplanes* © 1988 by E. Richard Churchill

© 2008 by Sterling Publishing Co., Inc.
Distributed in Canada by Sterling Publishing
*c/o* Canadian Manda Group, 165 Dufferin Street
Toronto, Ontario, Canada M6K 3H6
Distributed in the United Kingdom by GMC Distribution Services
Castle Place, 166 High Street, Lewes, East Sussex, England BN7 1XU
Distributed in Australia by Capricorn Link (Australia) Pty. Ltd.
P.O. Box 704, Windsor, NSW 2756, Australia

*Printed in China*
*All rights reserved*

Sterling ISBN 978-1-4027-6032-7

For information about custom editions, special sales, premium and
corporate purchases, please contact Sterling Special Sales
Department at 800-805-5489 or specialsales@sterlingpublishing.com.

# Contents

# Getting Started

Making and flying paper airplanes is fabulous fun. A sheet of paper, a few folds, and a minute or two are all you need to get started. From then on, the sky's the limit as you build and fly the paper airplanes described in this book. Soon you'll move on to designs and changes of your own.

A sheet of notebook paper will get you started. Just in case you're someone who likes to plan ahead, here's a list of supplies you'll be using as you build these airplanes. You won't use every item on each airplane, however.

1. **Paper:** This kit comes with cool paper to use for the planes. If you run out, notebook paper makes great airplanes. Typing paper or computer pages will also work perfectly.
2. **Scissors:** Sometimes you'll need to make cuts.
3. **Paper clips:** You'll use these to get your paper airplane in proper balance for great flights.
4. **Tape:** Cellophane tape is easy to use. Small strips of masking tape will work just as well (most of the time).
5. **Glue or staples:** Sometimes you'll want to use glue or staples instead of tape.
6. **Ruler:** Sometimes you'll need to do a bit of measuring.
7. **Pencil:** Dots and lines help with some of the airplanes.

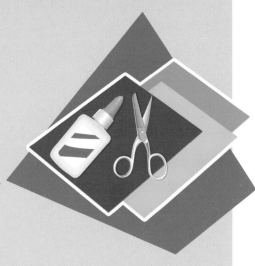

Some of the paper airplanes you'll be folding begin with a square sheet of paper. Take a few seconds to learn to turn a rectangular sheet of paper into a square sheet of paper.

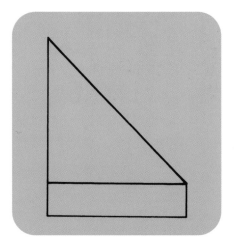

Begin by folding one corner of the paper over.

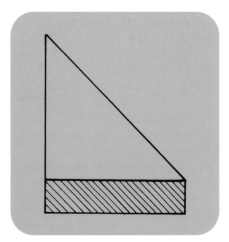

Cut away the shaded part of paper. When you unfold the paper, you'll have a perfectly square sheet.

# Flight School

Pilots spend many hours in flight school before they're qualified to fly an airplane. In flight school future pilots learn the basics of aviation—how an airplane flies and what they need to do in order to fly an airplane safely and well.

Even after earning a license and flying airplanes across the nation or even around the world, pilots still return to school for refresher courses from time to time.

This section is the reader's pilot flight school. You'll learn why fabulous *paper* airplanes fly and how to make them fly better. Let's begin by learning how an airplane flies, and how various parts of the aircraft help it to fly. Then we'll move on to turning the folded paper airplanes into great flying machines.

Read enough of this section to understand exactly how airplanes fly. Then fold and fly several of the airplanes in the book. Then come back to "flight school" and read a bit more. Read how the different parts of airplanes affect the plane's flight. Begin to use the technical terms when you discuss your paper airplanes. Put to use what you learn in flight school as you fold and fly more paper airplanes.

Finish flight school by reading about what you can do to correct or change the way your paper airplanes fly. Put this knowledge to work as you keep on folding and flying new and different paper airplanes.

Don't worry if you can't remember all the terms at first. "Flight school" will always be here for you—you can turn back to it from time to time.

## How Airplanes Fly

Four forces influence the way airplanes fly. The drawing shown below names these four forces. The arrows in the drawing show how each force acts upon an airplane. These four forces work on every airplane in the world, from commercial airlines to paper airplanes.

An airplane must have power to move forward. **Thrust** is the term pilots use when talking about power. Jets provide thrust for huge airliners. The force of your hand and your arm gives a paper airplane its needed thrust.

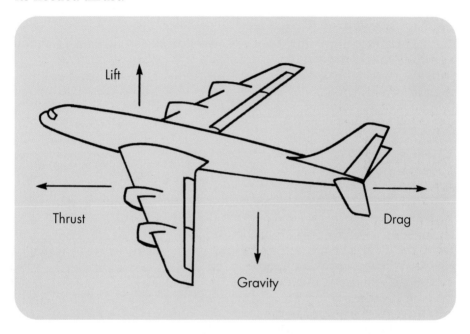

Lift

Thrust

Drag

Gravity

*Lift* is the second force that helps keep the airplane flying. An airplane's wings provide lift. As air moves across the curved surface on top of an airplane's wing, it creates an area of low pressure. This low air pressure provides lift. The air pressure beneath the wing is normal because the underside of the wing is not curved like the top of the wing.

Every airplane (whether powered by jets or by the force of your arm) has to overcome *drag* in order to fly. The pressure of the air through which the airplane flies creates drag. Drag slows down flight. The more of the plane's surface that is exposed to air, the greater the drag becomes. When an airplane's nose comes up it exposes more of the craft's surface to the air, increasing drag. If there is too much drag for the thrust and lift to overcome, the plane stalls, and it may even crash.

The fourth force acting on airplanes is *gravity.* Gravity's pull affects all things, including airplanes in flight. An aircraft has to overcome gravity's pull by combining lift and thrust in order just to get off the ground. Then gravity must still be overcome in order for the airplane to actually fly.

**Thrust and lift combined have to be greater than the total forces of drag and gravity in order for an airplane to fly.**

Now let's really get into "flight school" and learn how pilots talk and what the terms mean.

The first term all pilots need to know is *fuselage.* The fuselage is the body of the aircraft. It is that part of the airplane the wings and tail section are attached to.

Now let's move on to the *control surfaces.* Any movable part of an airplane's wings or its tail assembly is a control surface. Any time you change or adjust any control surface, there will be a difference in the way the airplane flies.

This illustration will serve as your introduction to our discussion of an airplane's wings.

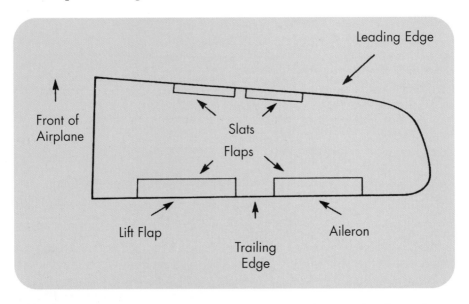

To begin with, the front of an airplane's wing is the *leading edge.* (This is easy to remember—the leading edge *leads* the wing through the air.) The wing's *trailing edge* follows or *trails* the wing. The trailing edge is the rear edge of the wing.

Any movable control surface on the wing's trailing edge may be called a *flap.* Flaps may be pointed down to increase the curve in the airplane's wing and thereby increase the lift. You increase lift on your paper airplane by folding or bending or rolling the trailing edge of the wing down slightly.

Pilots call some of the flaps *ailerons.* Aviation engineers and pilots know that air moves faster over a curved surface than over a flat surface. The faster the air moves, the greater the lift the air supplies. During takeoff and when climbing during flight, pilots adjust the ailerons to give more lift. The ailerons are extended out from the wing and pushed downward at an angle. This gives the wing more of a curved shape and it also provides extra lift.

Some of the larger airplanes have *lift flaps* along the wing's trailing edge. These lift flaps are closer to the fuselage than the ailerons. The purpose of the lift flap is to give even more lift during takeoff. When climbing, pilots tip the lift flaps downward to give extra lift.

Special control surfaces on the leading edge of the wings of large airplanes are known as *slats.* These slats may be adjusted during takeoff to provide the wing with even more lift.

This illustration shows an airplane head-on. The tips of the wings are higher than the spot where the wings join the fuselage. This upward angle is called *dihedral.* The amount of dihedral affects both lift and the way the airplane flies.

Some airplanes have drooping wings—the wing tips are lower than the spot where the wing joins the fuselage. Airplanes with this type of wing are said to have *negative dihedral.*

If you really want to let people know that you're a "flying school" graduate, mention a wing's *camber.* Camber refers to the curve *on top* of the wing that increases the speed of air flow *over* the wing.

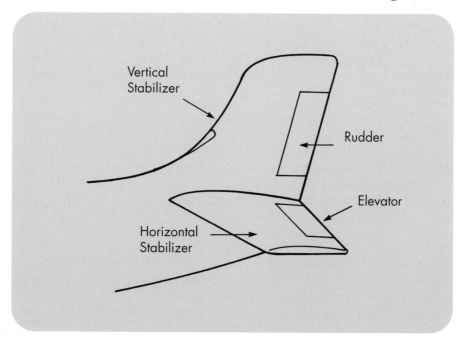

Let's now move back to the tail assembly. The illustration on page 9 shows you the basic tail portion of an airplane. Let's talk about the part of the tail extending outward from both sides of the fuselage (like little wings). This part is called the *horizontal stabilizer.* It's *horizontal* because it sticks out to the sides. It's a *stabilizer* because it helps keep the airplane stable or steady during flight.

The front of the horizontal stabilizer is its leading edge; the rear of the stabilizer is the trailing edge.

The control flap at the trailing edge of the horizontal stabilizer is known as the *elevator.* When it moves up or down it causes the airplane to gain or lose elevation.

The part of the tail section sticking straight up from the fuselage is the *vertical stabilizer.* It stands up *vertically* and it also helps to keep the airplane's flight *stable.*

The control flap at the trailing edge of the vertical stabilizer is called the *rudder.* The pilot moves the rudder to assist in turning the airplane during flight.

You don't have to remember all of these terms in order to fold and fly a paper airplane, but why not use the names pilots and aviation experts use? It helps to be exact when discussing aviation, and it's pretty impressive as well.

## Flying Your Fabulous Paper Airplanes

Now that you can talk about parts of your airplane like a commercial pilot, it's time to learn the vocabulary of flight itself.

Before we start, let's take a few seconds to discuss safety. Pilots are aware of the need for constant attention to safety while flying. You should be aware of safety as well, especially when flying your fabulous paper airplanes outdoors.

Here's a *safety tip.* When you take your paper airplanes outside, some will end up on housetops or in trees. When this happens, don't try to rescue your paper airplane. Wait for the wind to bring your plane down. Meanwhile, just go inside and fold a new one—it will take only a minute or two.

*Never* chase a paper airplane into the street. If your plane lands in the street, check for cars before even *thinking* about going for the airplane. If a car runs over your airplane, don't worry about it—just fold a new one.

With safety in mind, let's begin to speak like aviators as we fly our paper airplanes.

All flights begin with a launch. Launching puts your airplane into the air. A quick flick of the wrist gets some airplanes flying. Others prefer a gentle movement of your entire hand. When you launch airplanes outside, you'll often find that they need a little more force to launch them than if you launch them indoors.

One of the first words you'll need to know is *stall.* When an airplane hesitates, or almost stops in midair, it has gone into a stall.

The stalled plane will then flutter to the ground. Pilots have warning lights to let them know when a stall is coming—they can then prevent it.

If your airplane stalls, you probably need to adjust its **trim.** Trim means balancing an airplane so that it flies properly. Slip a paper clip or two onto the fuselage near the nose to correct most stalls. You'll find that moving one or more clips closer to the nose or toward the tail is often all you have to do to correct the trim and to have a smooth flight.

The opposite of a stall is a **dive.** A plane goes into a dive when there is too much weight near the front. Moving any paper clips toward the tail is an easy way to overcome a dive.

You can also prevent stalls and dives by bending or rolling the control surfaces on the trailing edges of the wings either up or down. Don't be afraid to experiment. Feel free to change control surfaces; learn what flight differences result from the various changes you make.

When you experiment with changes affecting your airplane's trim, try giving the wings on some airplanes more or less dihedral. This often changes their trim enough to affect the way they fly.

Some other quick trimming tips can change the flight characteristics of your fabulous paper airplanes. Try bending down the elevators on the trailing edges of the horizontal stabilizer if your airplane stalls. This tip, along with a paper clip on the nose, usually can cure stalling. If you make an airplane with the stabilizer and the wing in one piece, bend a small section of the wing's trailing edge. You can always make a pair of cuts in the trailing edge to create a small control flap. This technique works for wings or for a horizontal stabilizer.

You must do just the *opposite* to prevent dives. Lighten the nose or bend control surfaces *up* on the horizontal stabilizer to correct diving.

Paper airplanes often *bank* in flight, meaning that they turn either to the right or to the left. If your airplane banks, and you prefer a straight flight, here's what to do. Bend the aileron or the trailing edge of the wing downward on the side the plane is banking to. You can also bend *up* the opposite aileron or trailing edge. Or, you can do both. If your plane banks to the right, bend down the right aileron or bend up the left one.

You can also bend the trailing edge of the rudder in the opposite direction of the bank. A plane banking to the right can be corrected by bending the rudder or the trailing edge of the vertical stabilizer to the left.

Try these trimming tips and see what each one does to the airplane's flight characteristics. Don't be afraid to experiment.

Learn how trim changes affect flight characteristics. Work for smooth and level flights with some airplanes. Other airplanes are better suited for fast, straight flights. Some airplanes do better with slow, looping flights.

Pilots talk about *pitch* or *degree of pitch* when the airplane's nose goes up or down. Extreme pitch often causes stalling or diving. Paper clips on the fuselage cure pitch quickly.

When one wing tips to one side or to the other during flight, your airplane is *rolling.* First make certain that both wings have the same dihedral. Make sure that the trailing edges of both wings have the same amount of bending or folding; both should provide equal lift. You could *deliberately* cause your paper airplane to roll by setting the flaps or bending the trailing edges at different angles.

If your airplane's nose turns to the right or to the left, it is *yawing.* Yawing is often caused when the vertical stabilizer is not straight up and down. Check the vertical stabilizer first if your plane develops a yaw.

You may want to give a vertical stabilizer to an airplane that yaws. Just cut out a vertical stabilizer from a file card or very light cardboard and glue or tape the stabilizer into place. Be sure the stabilizer points straight up and down.

You can make your airplane perform a 360° roll in flight. Just adjust the control surfaces until the plane spins completely around on its axis without crashing.

*Inside loops* are great fun. A loop is a 360° loop or circle—the plane then goes on flying. To fly an inside loop, adjust the control surfaces so that the nose comes up and keeps on coming up, forcing the airplane to finish the loop.

The *outside loop* is when the airplane's nose goes down and the plane performs a complete loop or circle. Outside loops are harder to accomplish than inside loops, and are extremely dangerous to the pilots who attempt them.

Once you've mastered trimming, it's time to think about having some competition with other paper-airplane fliers. One of the most popular competition categories is *total distance covered in a single flight.* Be fair when flying outdoors—the wind must be the same for all flights.

Acrobatic-flying contests include loops, spins, banks, and rolls. Go for the most loops, the greatest banking, or the biggest number of direction changes during a single flight.

Congratulations! You have just graduated from flight school. Go out and have a *fabulous* flight!

# Dart

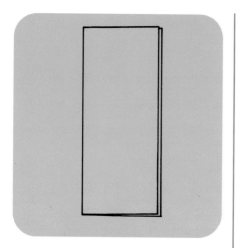

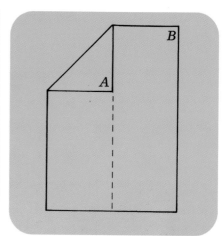

1. Begin by folding paper in half the long way. To make sure the fold stays in place, take just a second and crease it. An easy way to do this is to press the back of your thumbnail down firmly and run it along the fold.

2. Open the paper back up and fold corner A down to the center line. Crease the fold with your thumbnail so it looks like the illustration.

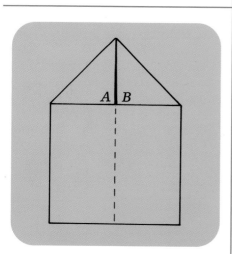

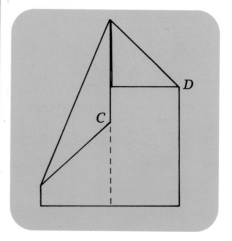

3. Fold corner B down to the center line. Take a second and crease this fold with your thumbnail.

4. Fold corner C over to the center line and crease the fold.

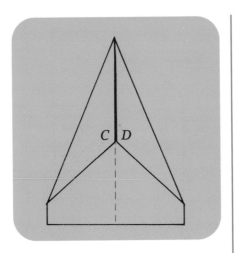

**5.** Fold and crease corner D.

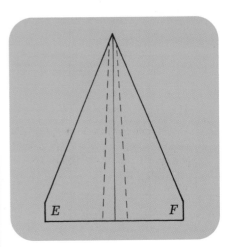

**6.** Turn the paper over and fold side E along the dotted line. Crease the fold; then unfold side E and crease side F along the dotted line.

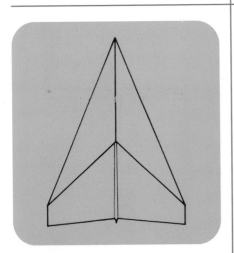

**7.** Unfold side F and turn the Dart over. Grasp the plane's body firmly between your thumb and forefinger. As you do this, the Dart's wings will lift and flatten out. Hold the plane's body between your thumb and forefinger and give the Dart a quick flick of your wrist. It should fly fast and straight, just like a dart.

# Variation

To make the plane that comes with the kit, try this variation. Complete steps 1–3 of the Dart, and then turn the plane over. Complete steps 4 and 5, and then fold each side in to the center and unfold. Fold the corners of the wing tips up to meet the crease line, turn the plane over, and grasp the body as you would the Dart.

# Little Dart

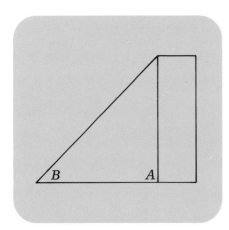

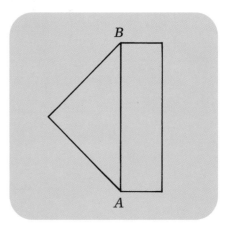

1. Fold corner A of paper over to the opposite side of the paper, and crease the fold.

2. Fold corner B over and crease it.

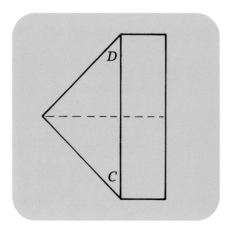

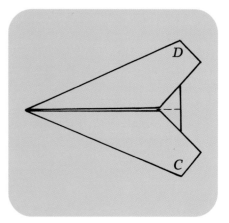

3. Fold the right side over to the left side, crease this fold, and then unfold.

4. Now fold side C over to the center; then fold side D to the center as well.

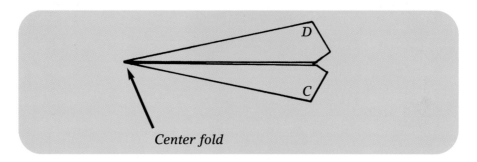

*Center fold*

5. Now fold in half along the center fold already in place. Fold side C down to the center. Turn over and fold side D down to the center.

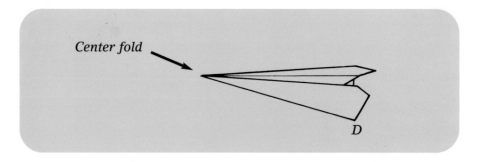

*Center fold*

D

6. Let the wings spread when you pick up the Little Dart. Take a firm grip on the fuselage and launch with a quick flick of the wrist.

# Little Wonder

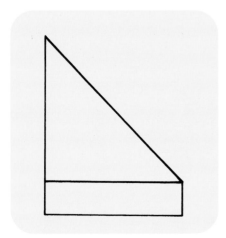

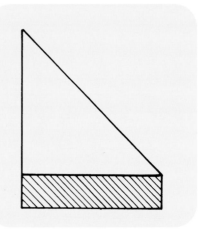

1. Square off paper: Fold the top right corner of the paper down to the opposite edge.

2. Cut off the paper shown by the slanted lines. When you unfold the paper, you will have a square sheet of paper.

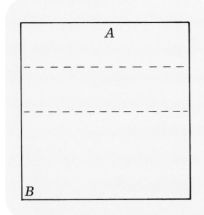

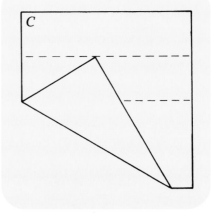

3. Fold the paper in half, crease the fold, and unfold. Now fold side A down to the center line, and unfold this crease as well.

4. Fold corner B up so that it exactly reaches the top fold. Make sure the fold starts at the left end of the center fold.

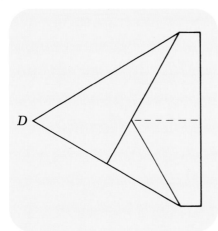

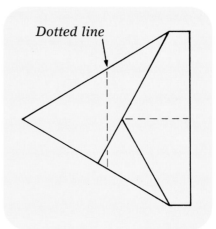

5. Now fold corner C down. Make sure the fold comes right down over corner B.

6. Next fold the pointed end D along the dotted line so that the point is exactly even with the center fold at the right hand side of the paper; then unfold it.

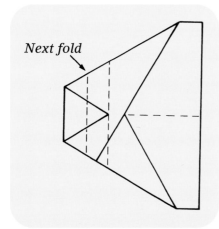

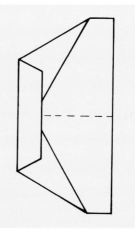

7. Now fold point D so that the point touches the crease you made in the last step; do not unfold. Crease the next fold along the dotted line indicated so that the edge of the paper comes right to the crease already in place.

8. Make one more fold on the plane's nose along the crease that is already there. Fold the wings together along the center fold.

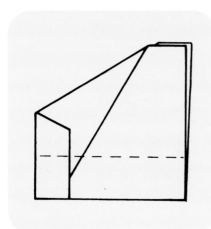

9. Along the dotted line, fold the nearest wing down; turn the plane over and fold the other wing down in the same way.

10. Open the wings and grasp the thick part of the fuselage right behind the nose. Give it a quick toss.

# Easy Glide

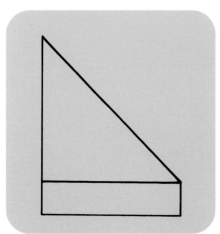

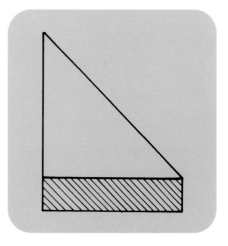

1. Square off paper: Fold the top right corner of the paper down to the opposite edge.

2. Cut off the paper shown by the slanted lines. When you unfold the paper, you will have a square sheet of paper.

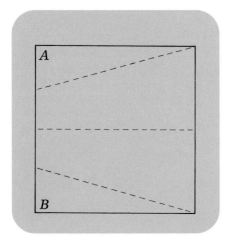

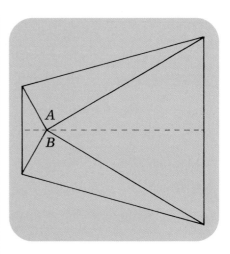

3. Fold one side of the paper over to the other and crease the fold. Now unfold the paper. Fold corners A and B along the dotted lines. Make sure A and B come exactly to the center fold.

4. Completed step 3.

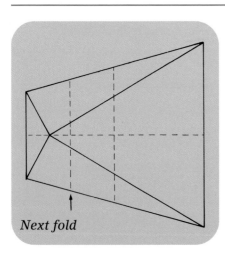

*Next fold*

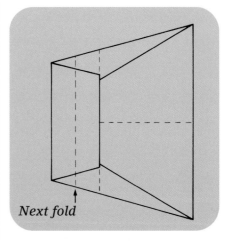

*Next fold*

5. Fold the nose of the airplane back to the tail; crease and unfold. Fold the nose over the next fold line so that it just touches the fold you made.

6. Fold the nose again over the dotted line; then fold the nose one more time along the crease you have been using as a guide.

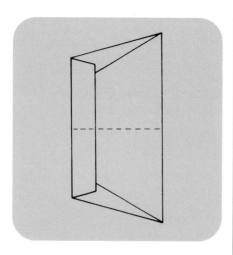

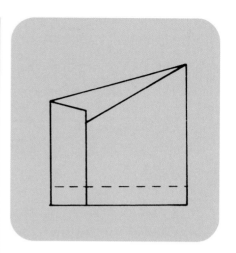

7. Fold your airplane in half along the center line.

8. Now fold the wings down, using the dotted line as a guide. Fold and crease the front wing down along the dotted line first; then turn over and fold down the second wing. Lift the wings into place.

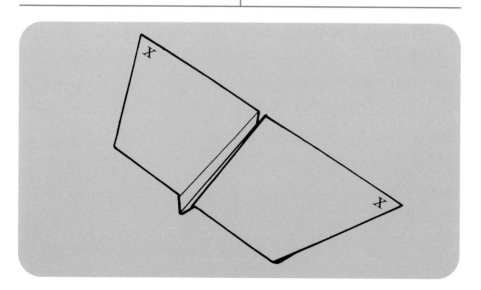

9. Gently bend (don't fold) the wings up so that the corners of the wings where the X's are turn upward slightly. Launch with a smooth movement of your hand.

# Playground
# Favorite

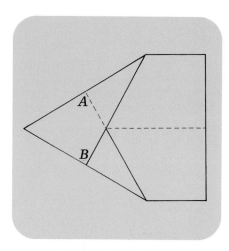

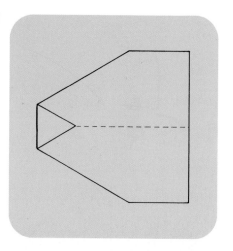

1. Fold paper lengthwise in the center to get a center crease; unfold. Fold corner A (make certain the fold begins right at the center crease). Fold corner B the same way.

2. Turn plane over and fold the nose back about $1\frac{2}{3}$ inches. Now fold the airplane upward along the center fold.

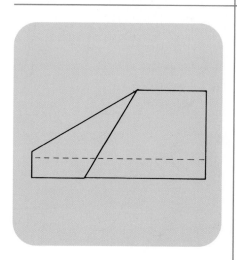

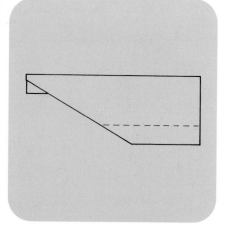

3. Fold the wing nearest you down along the dotted line and crease it into place; turn over and fold down the other wing.

4. Fold the wing nearest you up along the dotted line; then turn the airplane over and fold the other wing. Straighten the wings upward and launch with a quick snap of your arm and wrist.

# School Yard Special

1. Fold paper in half the long way. Fold corner A down to meet the previous fold and crease it into place. Turn the plane over and fold down the other front corner as well.

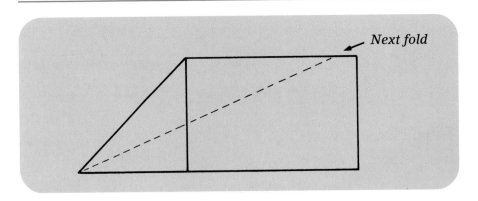

2. Fold the wing nearest you down and crease along the dotted line; turn the plane over and do the same for the other wing.

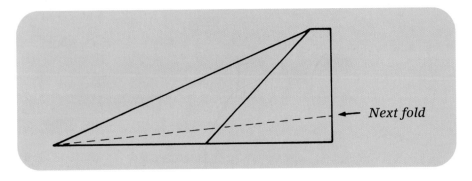

3. Fold the wings along the dotted line. Note that this line is slanted up from the point of the nose. Straighten the wings back up.

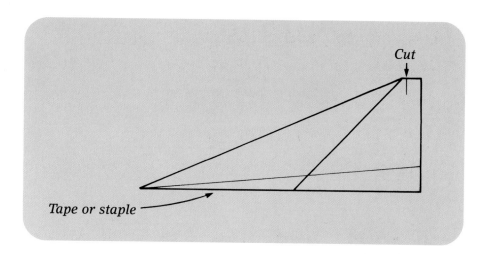

Tape or staple

**4.** Use a piece of tape or a staple to fasten the loose edges together at the bottom of the fuselage. Cut the slit in each wing.

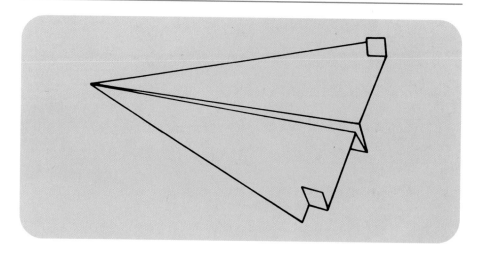

**5.** Flatten the wings into place; then fold up the two pieces you made with the two cuts. These are the vertical stabilizers.

# Perfect

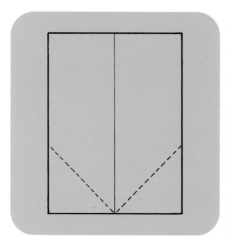 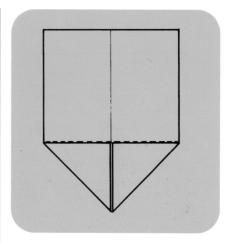

1. Begin by folding your paper down the middle the long way. Unfold it and lay it flat. Fold each corner right to the middle line along the two dotted lines.

2. Fold up along the dotted line.

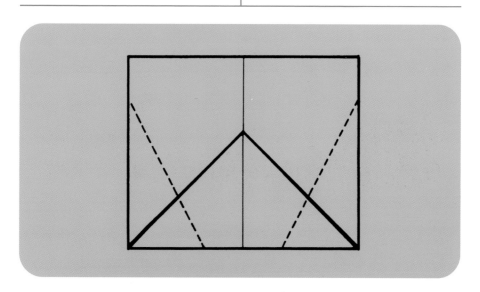

3. Make the two folds as indicated so that the corners of the paper come together exactly at the middle line.

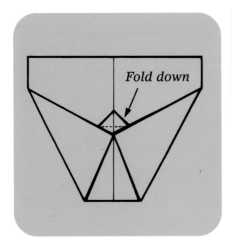

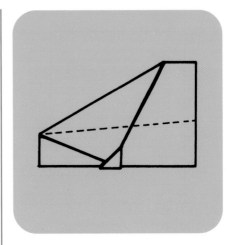

4. Make the fold along the dotted line. When this fold is made, fold Perfect along its middle line.

5. The dotted line shown indicates where to make the wing folds; fold down the wing nearest you along the dotted line. Turn the airplane over and fold down the second wing so it matches the first. The plane is now ready to fly.

# Bulldog

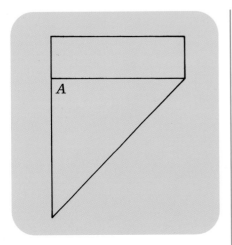 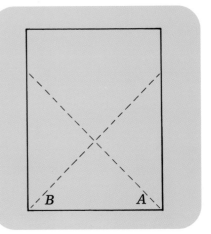

1. Begin by folding corner A over to the opposite side. Unfold. Next fold corner B over to its opposite corner, crease, and unfold.

2. Turn the paper over. Fold corners A and B up so that they meet the creases at the top of the paper.

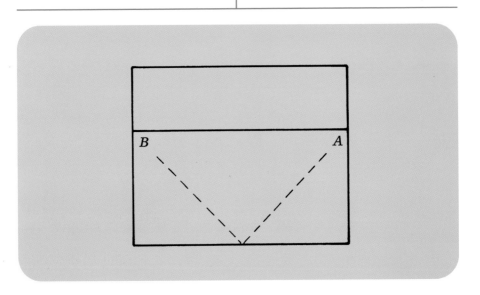

3. Unfold all the folds and turn the paper over again.

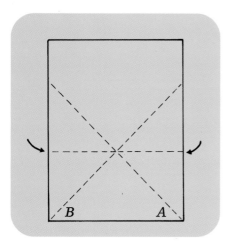

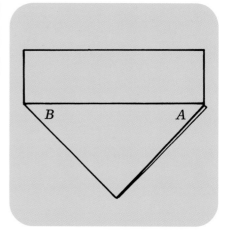

4. Push in the paper as shown by the arrows. As you push the paper together, the bottom corners A and B will lift up and the two arrows should come together.

5. Fold corner A down and crease it into place, folding down only the first two layers of paper. Now fold corner B in the same way.

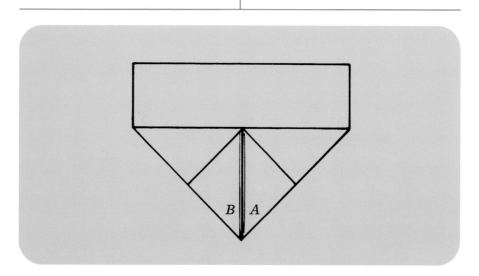

6. Fold the nose back and crease it firmly. Fold the paper in half.

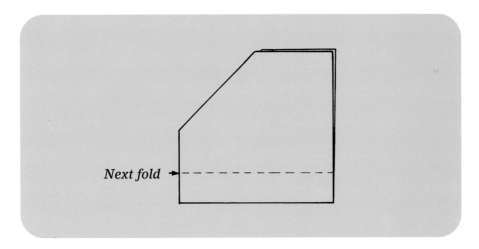

*Next fold*

7. Fold the wing nearest you down along the dotted line and crease that fold; turn the Bulldog over and fold down the other wing to match the first wing. Spread the wings open and it is ready for flight.

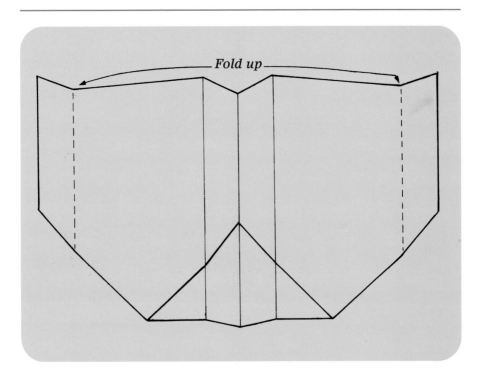

*Fold up*

8. If you'd like, try folding the outer edges of the wings upward along the dotted lines.

# Hawk

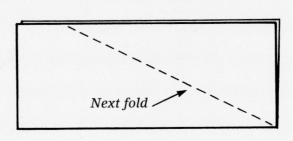

*Next fold*

1. Begin by folding a sheet of paper in half lengthwise. Turn the paper so the fold is up and toward you. Measure $1\frac{2}{3}$ inches in from the left on the upper side and mark that point with a small dot. Fold on dotted line.

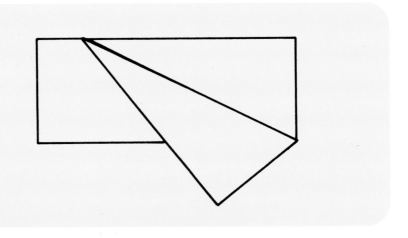

2. Completed step 1.

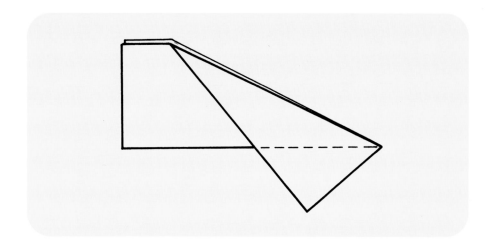

3. Turn the airplane over and fold the other side so it matches the previous fold. Fold the Hawk up along the dotted line. Turn the airplane over and fold the other side up in the same manner.

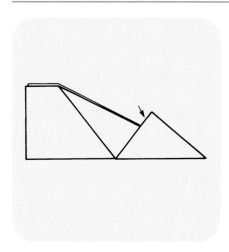

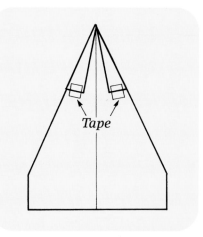

Tape

4. After making the last folds, there is some extra material extending past the airplane, as shown by the arrow.

5. Open the airplane and fold the extra material back over the rest of the airplane. Use a bit of cellophane tape to hold each of these flaps in place.

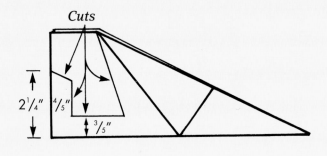

**Cuts**

$2\frac{1}{4}''$  $\frac{4}{5}''$  $\frac{3}{5}''$

6. Refold the Hawk down its middle fold. Use a pencil and ruler to draw the cut lines shown in the illustration. Cut along the lines while the paper is folded. Be sure you hold the two halves of the paper firmly together so that the Hawk is exactly the same on both sides.

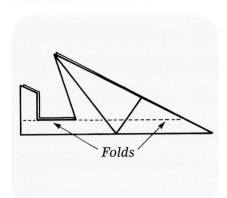

**Folds**

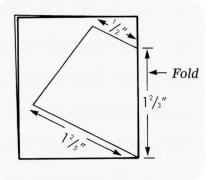

$\frac{1}{2}''$  **Fold**  $1\frac{2}{3}''$  $1\frac{2}{5}''$

7. Fold both the wings and the horizontal stabilizer down along the dotted lines.

8. Fold a separate small piece of paper in half and draw the vertical portion of the tail so it looks like the drawing above. Make sure the fold is on the side indicated. Draw the dimensions indicated to create the vertical stabilizer and cut. Slip the vertical stabilizer into place (in the fold) with the folded side facing forward. The rear of the vertical stabilizer extends about $\frac{1}{10}$ inch beyond the fuselage.

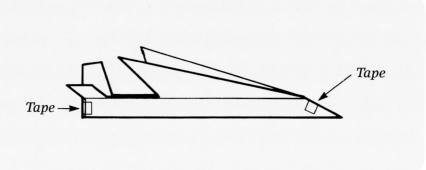

Tape

Tape →

9. Use a bit of cellophane tape to hold the nose together. Then tape the rear of the fuselage to hold the vertical stabilizer in place.

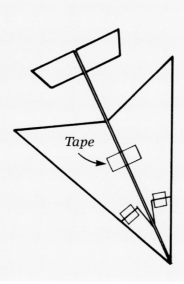

Tape

10. Pull the wings together with a strip of tape. Give the wings some dihedral: Place one end of the tape on the right-hand wing and press it firmly into place at the point shown in the illustration. Don't let the other end of the tape touch the paper yet. Lift the tips of the wings so that they are $^3/_4$ inch higher than the point where the wings join the fuselage. Press the loose end of the tape on the left-hand wing. The tape will hold the wings up and give the plane its dihedral. Launch it with a smooth forward motion of your hand and arm.

# Steady Glide

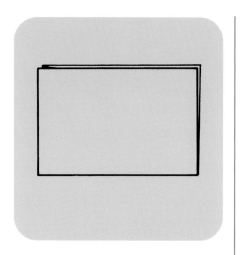

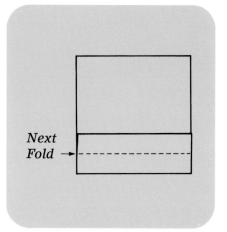

1. Fold paper in half the short way.

2. Unfold previous fold. Fold the bottom of the paper up, so that the bottom edge touches the middle fold. Crease this second fold. Fold along the dotted line.

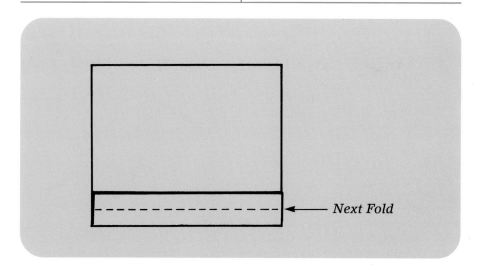

*Next Fold*

3. Completed step 2. Make the fold along the dotted line. Then turn and fold the airplane in half. Crease this fold.

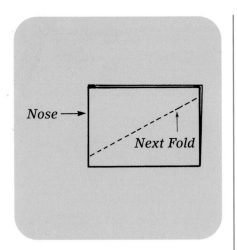

4. Fold along the dotted line to make a wing. This fold should start and end $\frac{1}{2}$ inch from the corners of the paper.

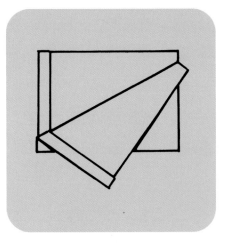

5. Completed step 4. Turn the airplane over and fold down the second wing exactly as you did the first wing.

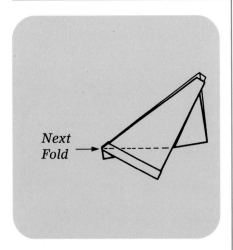

6. The next fold makes the point of the folded paper run uphill toward the airplane's nose. Fold up the wing closer to you along the dotted line. Turn the airplane over and fold the second wing exactly as you did the first.

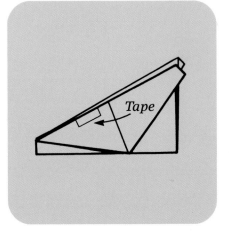

7. Use a small strip of tape to hold this last fold tightly in place. After taping one wing, do the same on the other wing.

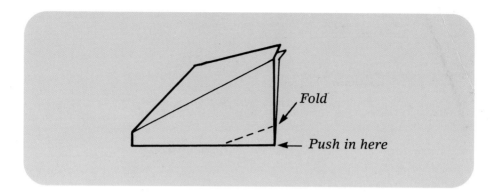

*Fold*

*Push in here*

8. Lift wings up and out of the way. Fold the fuselage toward you, along the dotted line. Fold the fuselage back away from you, along the fold you just made. Hold the airplane in one hand and hold the fuselage with the other hand at the point shown by the arrow. Push up on the end of the fuselage and turn the folded part inside out. When you're finished, the folded area will stick up inside the fuselage where it will act as a vertical stabilizer.

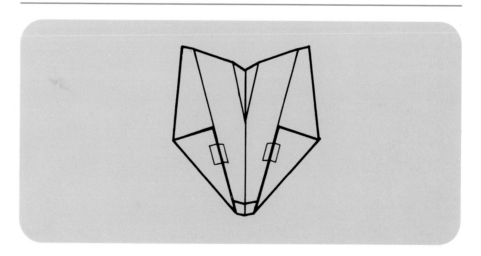

9. Completed Steady Glide. Launch with a steady, forward movement of your hand and arm.

# Index